John Lewis-Stempel is the author of *Meadowland*, winner of the 2015 Thwaites Wainwright Prize for Nature Writing, and *The Running Hare*, a *Sunday Times* Top 10 bestseller. He was Magazine Columnist of the Year in 2016 for his notes on farming and nature in *Country Life*.

www.**penguin**.co.uk

The
Secret Life
of the
OWL

John Lewis-Stempel

Doubleday

LONDON · NEW YORK · TORONTO · SYDNEY · AUCKLAND

TRANSWORLD PUBLISHERS
61–63 Uxbridge Road, London W5 5SA
www.penguin.co.uk

Transworld is part of the Penguin Random House group of companies
whose addresses can be found at global.penguinrandomhouse.com

Penguin
Random House
UK

First published in Great Britain in 2017 by Doubleday
an imprint of Transworld Publishers

Illustrations by Beci Kelly

A CIP catalogue record for this book
is available from the British Library.

ISBN 9780857524560

Typeset in 11/14.5pt Goudy Old Style
Printed and bound by Clays Ltd, Bungay, Suffolk.

Penguin Random House is committed to a sustainable
future for our business, our readers and our planet. This book
is made from Forest Stewardship Council® certified paper.

5 7 9 10 8 6 4

The Owls

Among the black yews, their shelter,
the owls are ranged in a row,
like alien deities, the glow
of their red eyes pierces. They ponder.
They perch there without moving,
till that melancholy moment
when quenching the falling sun,
the shadows are growing.
Their stance teaches the wise
to fear, in this world of ours,
all tumult, and all movement:
Mankind drunk on brief shadows
always incurs a punishment
for his longing to stir, and go.

Charles Baudelaire (1821–67),
translated by A. S. Kline

CONTENTS

Prologue: The Owl in the Wood *1*

Introduction: O is for Owl *3*

I: What is an Owl? *9*

II: The Owls of Britain *27*

III: Humans and Owls *61*

Epilogue: The Lord of the Night *81*

British and International Owl Societies *85*

The Owl in the Wood

THE TAWNY OWL in Three Acre Wood sometimes glides over my head as he takes an evening circuit. (The animals, like us, have their rituals.) There are times when he comes within three feet – two even? – and I cannot tell, so quiet is his flight . . . except for a slight weightiness in the air around me. This is at twilight, so when I look up, I see his stub of shadow in the sky. At night when he passes overhead he is subtext, something present but unseen.

We farm pigs, sheep and cattle to the edge of the wood (and sometimes in it), so Old Brown and I are well acquainted. I go about my business, he about his. To be accepted by an owl you must be a familiar in the scene. Owls are fearful of the new.

Old Brown likes to sit on an ornamental, twist-barked chestnut tree just inside the wood. I walked up to him last week, in evening's fire-glow, and he observed my approach with professorial focus. Birds know intention. So I kept my hands in my coat pockets, to prove the *pax*. I suppose he let me approach to within ten feet, until he flew off on his slow, moth wings; the lord of the night. There was no alarm. He had simply lost interest, and had better things to do than spend time human-watching.

I, on the other hand, had no greater want than to go owl-watching.

O is for Owl

Howl.
The word owl goes back to the *ule* of Anglo-Saxon times, and has equivalents across Europe (French *hibou*, German *Eule*, Dutch *uil*, Latin *ulula*), all of them derived from some root-word used by the Ancients to denote and imitate the cry of the wolf. Like the howling wolf, the howling owl is a creature of the night, thus of magic.

Night is when evil deeds are done. Accordingly, no witch's potion has ever been complete without a portion of owl (in Shakespeare's *Macbeth*, Act IV, the witches famously want a wing of 'howlet'), no Gothic novel finished without an owl's ghostly hooting, no horror flick ended without a big close-up of an owl's staring eyes. Even such a consummate twentieth-century literary technician as Sylvia Plath was unable to resist a dab of 'pale, raptorial' owl in her poetry to suggest the menace possessing a New England town.

Night is desolation, and so is the habitat the owl makes its resort. The prophet Isaiah foresaw the overthrow of Babylon, after which, amid the wasteland, 'owls shall dwell there'. Owls belong to ruins, woods and moors. Truly, they are wild birds.

Owls carry out their lives when we, diurnal beings, are asleep. Nocturnality is as rare in birds as it is in humans; less than 3 per cent of avians work after sunset.

Owls, then, are Other. They are beyond the pale of light, civilization, goodness. When the medieval English needed a neologism for the crime of the midnight smuggling of wool fleeces to France, what did they invent? 'Owling'.

Poor owls. If they do venture to fly by day, this bodes ill, because it is the natural order turned upside down. Shakespeare in *Julius Caesar* had a daytime owl portend Caesar's end:

> *Yesterday the bird of night did sit,*
> *Even at noonday, upon the market place,*
> *Hooting and shrieking.*

And yet the owl is also a positive favourite in the nursery. The owl, depicted as kindly and sagacious (if unable to spell), is Wol in A. A. Milne's Pooh stories, the bookish Wise Owl in Alison Uttley's Little Grey Rabbit saga, and the co-star of Edward Lear's nonsense poem, 'The Owl and the Pussy-cat'.

With its upright stance, big eyes and large sapiens-similar face the owl is easily anthropomorphized (and manufactured into a cuddly toy). Even die-hard ornithologists, when they encounter *Athene noctua*, the little owl, see a stern parental expression on its face. Snowy owls have the demeanour of disdainful ice kings and queens. Tawnies, like Wol, look gruffly benevolent.

There is something about owls. More than any other family of birds they produce a reaction in us, and have done so across time and continents. It is atavistic; we are genetically programmed to care for lookalikes. In ancient times the owl was known as the 'human-headed bird'. We fall for that manlike face.

I am writing this on the western edge of England in November, during that uncertain half-hour when day and night overlap as in a Venn diagram, when dusk is filling the valley like silt tide. Some call it the gloaming, others the 'owl-light'.

Out in the wood behind the house, our resident tawny owl has started calling.

Hoo-hoo-hoo-h-o-o-o.

Yes, Old Brown's call is ghostly. But it is also a benediction on the land; owls only hunt where there is life to kill.

So, to humans an owl is many things between Good and Bad. But what is an owl unto itself?

The Owl and the Pussy-cat

The Owl and the Pussy-cat went to sea
In a beautiful pea-green boat,
They took some honey, and plenty of money,
Wrapped up in a five-pound note.
The Owl looked up to the stars above,
And sang to a small guitar,
'O lovely Pussy! O Pussy, my love,
What a beautiful Pussy you are,
You are,
You are!
What a beautiful Pussy you are!'

Pussy said to the Owl, 'You elegant fowl!
How charmingly sweet you sing!
O let us be married! too long we have tarried:
But what shall we do for a ring?'
They sailed away, for a year and a day,
To the land where the Bong-tree grows
And there in a wood a Piggy-wig stood
With a ring at the end of his nose,
His nose,
His nose,
With a ring at the end of his nose.

'Dear Pig, are you willing to sell for one shilling
Your ring?' Said the Piggy, 'I will.'
So they took it away, and were married next day
By the Turkey who lives on the hill.
They dined on mince, and slices of quince,
Which they ate with a runcible spoon;
And hand in hand, on the edge of the sand,
They danced by the light of the moon,
The moon,
The moon,
They danced by the light of the moon.

Edward Lear (1812–88)

I

What is an Owl?

THE DICTIONARY DEFINITION of an owl is 'a nocturnal bird of prey'. Not absolutely all owls, however, are night birds; up on the black Welsh hills beyond our house, the short-eared owls regularly quarter (range up and down) the stunted, wind-whipped grass in broad daylight. Then there is the matter of size: the elf owl is Lilliputian and barely dents the scales at 47g, while Blakiston's fish owl is Brobdingnagian and nearly breaks them at 4,500g. There are white owls and brown owls. Owls that live on fish, owls that eat insects. Across Planet Earth there are currently around 225 different species of owl. Alas, the laughing owl of New Zealand is now extinct, one less thing for us to smile about.

Putting birds into scientific categories can be as fruitless as catching the wind with your hands. But it seems to be human habit. Aristotle separated birds into those that lived on water and those that lived alongside it. Nineteen hundred years later, in the seventeenth century, Francis Willughby wrote *Ornithologiae libri tres*, proposing a classification based on morphology, basic body shape. Carl Linnaeus (1707–78), 'the father of modern taxonomy', deposited owls in the same scientific order as hawks. More modern taxonomists postulate that hawks and owls are similar only because of 'convergent evolution', or nature finding the same solution via different routes. The latest state-of-the-science bends towards placing owls into their own unique order, the Strigiformes: from *strix*, the Greek for 'owl'. According to this owl-holing, there are two families of Strigiformes: the true owls, the *Strigidae*, and the barn owls, the *Tytonidae*.

The differences between *Strigidae* and *Tytonidae* are minor: barn owls have longer legs and relatively smaller eyes. At the end of the day, at the beginning of the night, and for all of the anguish of scientists . . . owls are owls. They are instantly recognizable. Owls have a big, domed head, a flat face, large forward-facing eyes and a hooked beak for tearing flesh. Male owls are generally smaller than the females, a characteristic more noticeable in owls that feed on vertebrates than on invertebrates. The degree of this 'size dimorphism' varies with the species; it is just 5 per cent in the barn owl but 25 per cent in the tawny. Dimorphism allows the female of the species to survive hard times.

Owls have no visible neck; the head apparently swivels on a covert mechanical axis. There are owls that can rotate their heads through 270 degrees; a human can manage 180, if that. Owls can also tilt their heads, up/down 90 degrees. Such flexibility is possible because owls have fourteen neck vertebrae, twice as many as a human being.

Owls have understated plumage, invariably brownish, and evolved (or designed) to allow each species to blend into its chosen habitat. While the majority of owls are tenants of the wood and the forest, they can also be found on terrains as opposite as Arctic tundra and African desert.

Curiously, the predacious owl chiefly requires camouflage to roost in peace. Owls are feared by other birds, and if spotted in daytime are attacked by even the tiniest passing passerine. 'The owl by day, / If he arise, be mock'd and wonder'd at', as Shakespeare, that keen observer of animal behaviour, noted in *Henry V*. When 'mobbing', antagonistic birds will dive-bomb the owl, claws extended, descending to within an inch of the owl's face.

Such is the compulsion for other birds to mob owls they will attack stuffed specimens of *Strigidae*, even wooden facsimiles. The owly silhouette is as distinctive to a bird as it is to us.

Over the millennia, humans have taken advantage of the mobbed owl to fill the stew pot. A Greek amphora from the sixth century BC shows an owl tethered to a post; a flock of birds has landed on an adjacent tree, the branches of which have been smeared with adhesive 'birdlime' to trap them. Two centuries later, in c.350 BC, Aristotle recorded the use of the owl as bait: 'In the daytime all the other little birds flutter round the owl – a practice which is popularly termed "admiring him" – buffet him, and pluck out his feathers; in consequence of this habit, bird-catchers use the owl as a decoy for catching little birds of all kinds.' An identical technique is depicted in the De Lisle Psalter of England, c.1310, where birds landing on a branch to mob a tethered owl get trapped by birdlime; in Britain this glue was usually concocted from boiled holly or wayfaring-tree bark, or mistletoe berries. The cockney rhyming slang 'doing bird', meaning time spent in prison, comes from 'birdlime' via 'doing time'.

Long-eared owls possess feather camouflage so effective that they can sleep against a tree trunk unseen, even by gangs of long-tailed tits working adjacent branches; the lack of neck further helps the deceit, because it enables the owl to perform an impression of a broken bough.

Can owls see in the dark? Nearly. When it is rat-black the iris of an owl's eye opens almost completely to allow in all the light there is. Also, the retina is crammed with rods, the receptors concerned with seeing in poor light conditions. (The rod:cone ratio is roughly 30:3.) As a result, a long-eared owl can see a mouse in a light level equivalent to one candle in a football stadium.

With this light-sensitive optical equipment Old Brown, as Beatrix Potter called the gnomic if frightening tawny owl in *The Tale of Squirrel Nutkin*, can fly around his familiar wood at night, although not under leaf canopy when it is wholly overcast. Fortunately, for tawnies and other night owls, there is always the subfusc of dawn and dusk.

Owls have the best 'stereoscopic' vision of all the birds. An owl's eyes almost fill its skull, taking up to 70 per cent of the available space.

A tawny has a skull the size of a golf ball, but eyes the size of a human child's. By having its eyes pointing forward, the owl is killer-efficient in determining distance and movement. But there is a drawback to the owl's supersized eyes, which are contained within rigid tubes (these extend beyond the skull, a feature observable in naked owlets, but in adults it is hidden by facial feathers). The eyes are immovable in the skull. An owl cannot roll its eyes, for example. When owls need to judge the position of an object they bob, or swivel, their head about.

There are times and seasons to watch for owls. That half-light at the beginning and the end of the day offers the best opportunity for watching, as opposed to merely hearing, the nocturnal owls, particularly in bitter winter weather when birds invariably extend their hunting time beyond darkness. Or try the raw December night, when the leaves are down and the moon is up, to look for tawnies in the wood or the park. Early winter is the prime time to hear tawnies, when they are staking their claim to territory. Follow the sound trail through the frosted air, perhaps for a mile or more. The length of the winter night means that the owl will call on and off for over twelve hours, and well past dawn. Our Old Brown will hoot as late as 7.45am in January.

A tawny advertising for land will often hoot from the same position night after night. Never use a torch. Unexpected bright lights temporarily blind the owl. After your eyes have become 'dark adapted', you will be pleasantly surprised by just how much light is out there. Be the bird.

Despite their deadly keen eyesight, owls can bungle the identification of stationary objects. When I was a teenager, I was standing watching a barn owl quarter the harvest field on a late and breathless July evening. The bird flew so low that its trailing legs skimmed the ears of wheat. It progressed as methodically up and down the field as Mike Hughes, the ploughman, had four months before. Then the owl veered to rest on the convenient post, which was me. Only when I shrieked did the owl swerve away, her witchy claws catching my hair as she did so.

We were both equally surprised by the close encounter.

When the eyes are not enough, such as for Old Brown in moonless autumn with the leaves still clinging to the trees, owls locate their prey by listening for movement. The ears of the owl are more marvellous even than its eyes.

In owls, the ears are set asymmetrically in their skulls, with one ear as much as 15 degrees further up the skull than the other, and sometimes of larger size. (A few owls have asymmetrical skulls too.) Asymmetrical positioning of the outer ears means that each ear receives sound at a slightly different volume and angle, which allows the owl to pinpoint where the sound comes from. There is also a flap of skin in front of the ear which the bird can control to catch sound, in the way that old gentlemen cup their hand to their ear. Indeed, the entire facial disc of the owl acts as an amplifier. More: the owl's brain also has a preponderance of nerve cells in the auditory area. A barn owl's brain has 95,000 neurons in the auditory region, compared with only 27,000 in the diurnal crows. In receiving sounds, owls are capable of detecting time differences of as little as 30 millionths of a second.

All this means that some nocturnal owls can kill by hearing alone. In total darkness. In blackout. Night is no friend to prey animals when an owl is about.

Hearing is most acute in the owls which hunt the northern forests, tundra and pasture, which are silent except for the whining of the wind and the faint rustle of small mammals in the grass and leaf litter. There is too much fauna noise in the steamy rainforest to make perfect hearing worthwhile.

The owl on the hunt, having located its prey, continues to listen throughout the approach, which is done on silent wings, partly to avert the alerting of prey, partly because loud wings would interfere with the bird's own hearing. The victim only becomes aware of the owl's presence as the talons close in deadly grip. Owls are the avian stealth predators.

Owls have special feathers to facilitate silent flight. Comb-like serrations on the leading edge of the wings and a velvety fringe on the trailing edge 'dampen' noise. Then there is the overall softness of the plumage; an owl in the hand is curiously fluffy. There are owl feathers that feel as fine as a baby's hair. The multitude of downy feathers make the owl look a lot larger than it really is; a long-eared owl has a 95cm wingspan but weighs the same as an orange.

The feathers grow down to the razor-slash claws, to protect the legs from bite-back prey (barn owls have been known to attack stoats, a foot-length of pure violence if ever there was one). Feathered legs also minimize heat loss, crucial to those wait-on-the-bough owl species, like tawnies, which lurk immobile for long periods waiting for prey to happen along.

The talons, which are arranged in a special foot design called zygodactylous ('paired toes'), in which two claws point forwards and two back, are the owl's primary weapons. They capture and kill the bird's prey. Prey is taken by the bird swooping from a perch, or from low quartering flight, between 0.5 and 2m above the ground. The momentum of the pounce or swoop adds to the weight of the owl and enables it to kill animals twice its size. In all instances the prey is struck with the feet pushed out in front of the bird, the talons fully open, to make a spring trap of claws. As the owl's talons slice in, then close, the prey dies from shock or the puncturing of a vital organ.

The evolution of the owl reaches its apogee in this moment: a perfect connect between targeting ear/eye and the striking talon.

If the prey is still somehow alive, a swift sharp nip from the owl's hooked bill will finish it off.

Owls are purist killers. Some avian predators, such as the peregrine, taunt their victim. In the battle of survival, the owl eschews posing for economy and efficiency. Owls are the men-at-arms at Agincourt, the Cromwellian horsemen at Marston Moor. They kill. Fly on. Kill. Fly on.

The quick dispatch saves time, which is energy, which is time. The owl is amoral concerning killing.

This is not to say that owls are without gentleness, though this is expressed to their kin, and those humans who adopt the birds. Owls make good pets. Florence Nightingale rescued an owlet from the Parthenon after it fell from its nest. She named the bird, a little owl, Athena and kept her as a companion. Athena would perch on her mistress's finger for feeds, as well as bow and curtsy on a table, and lived in Nightingale's pocket. When the beloved Athena died in 1855 Nightingale delayed her departure for nursing duties in the Crimea so she could arrange for the bird to be expertly embalmed. It is currently an exhibit at the Florence Nightingale Museum, London.

Pablo Picasso also kept a pet little owl, which lived with him in his studio in Paris. According to Françoise Gilot, Picasso's muse and lover, the owl 'smelled awful and ate nothing but mice. Since Pablo's atelier was overrun with them, I set several traps. Whenever I caught one, I brought it to the owl. As long as I was in the kitchen, he ignored the mouse and me. He saw perfectly well in the daytime, of course, in spite of the popular legend about owls, but he apparently preferred to remain aloof. As soon as I left the kitchen, even if only for a minute, the mouse disappeared.'

Picasso thought of himself as an owl, because of his staring eyes. An owl motif featured in many of his ceramics and paintings, famously, 'Owl on a Chair and Sea Urchins' from 1946, and 'Cage with Owl', 1947.

Owls are old. The oldest known record of an owl, the fossil *Ogygoptynx wetmorei*, is from about 58 million years ago.

There is present proof of the antiquity of owls. Most contemporary owls nest in holes in trees or cliffs or buildings and all have round, chalky-white eggs. The lack of markings on the eggs is a good indication that the owls have been cavity-nesting birds for millions of years; bird species that nest in the open invariably evolve pigmented eggs which serve as concealment, aid to parental recognition, or (as with the blue eggs of the thrush) the speeding up of embryonic development.

Nesting owls have the standard avian gender division of labour, whereby the male is responsible for most of the prey provision, the female responsible for care of the young at the nest. Female owls keep the eggs warm by contact with naked skin on her underside, a 'brood patch' where the veins enlarge to act as heat exchangers with the eggs. Radiators, in a word. Three to four eggs is the norm laid per clutch.

Young owls leave the nest before being capable of proper flight. Tawnies are fluff balls when they first clamber around the branches of the home tree. If they fall, they re-scale the tree by the hook of their bill and the crooks of their claws. It can take many weeks before the young can hunt alone. Eagle owls do not achieve independence from the parent until twenty-five to thirty weeks.

Creatures of the night, owls communicate primarily by sound. Calls are generally loud, carrying for as much as two miles over frosted ground. Territorial calls are the prerogative of the male, trumpeted into the night so females can seek who to breed with. Vocalization is a sign of breeding quality: the owl that sings loudest, longest is likely to be of better stock than one who can only afford to sing for short periods. Numerous owl species make hunting calls, which are sharp and explosive, designed to scare small mammals into movement whereby they can be seen, heard, killed. Apart, perhaps, from the bassoon 'hoos' of the tawny, owls could never be declared musical. Still, as the Danish proverb has it, 'If there are no nightingales, one must settle for owls.'

Owls are, by and large, monogamous, forming pair bonds that last at least one season. Sedentary species, such as tawny owls, little owls and eagle owls, may mate for a lifetime.

Owls can live for years. The oldest wild owl on record was a long-eared owl which totted up twenty-seven years. A British tawny reached twenty-one years, and a compatriot barn owl thirteen. However, the typical lifespan of British owls is three to four years.

In Britain the owl is top of the wild food chain. Well, almost. Goshawks, peregrines and buzzards are all known to have taken barn owls, tawnies and long-eared owls, while the little owl, given its size, is an unsurprising item in the diet of more than a dozen raptor species.

Night hides the owl, which is a slow flyer compared to other avian predators. Those soft wings make for little speed and hard work. One study found that 73 per cent of tawny owls which died from natural causes were killed by day birds of prey.

No wonder Old Brown generally prefers life at night.

The Pellets of Common British Owls

A feature of owls is their need to puke up pellets of indigestible food. Courtesy of clever biology, the pellet is formed in the owl's gizzard in such a way that sharper, bonier objects are enclosed by an outer mattress of rejected fur.

The production of pellets by the owl follows an unchanging cycle. The caught corpse, often swallowed whole, slides down the bird's throat and, since owls have no crop, straight into the glandular stomach (gizzard). The digestible parts of the meal are passed on to the intestines for absorption, while the indigestible parts are compacted into a pellet, which is stored in the gizzard for up to ten hours. During this phase of the digestive cycle the owl cannot feed because the pellet is blocking the gizzard. When the owl is ready to hunt again the pellet is coughed up, the bird closing its eyes and stretching its neck upwards and forwards. The pellet falls out of the owl's beak to the ground.

On being ejected by the owl, the pellet is damp and covered with mucus. Since owls have a narrow pyloric opening from the stomach to the intestines, all but the tiniest fragments of bone or other hard material is prevented from passing onwards from the stomach. Consequently, the regurgitated pellet contains virtually the complete skeletons of the prey devoured the night before.

Pellets vary in size, shape and structure according to the species of owl. Furry pellets are the original food larder for the clothes moths that eventually migrate to your wardrobe and mine.

Species	Size (mm)	Description of pellets
Tawny owl	30 – 70 × 10 – 20	Pale grey, felted, loose.
Barn owl	30 – 70 × 18 – 26	Black, compact, smooth, almost 'varnished' exterior when fresh. Often found in heaps in the buildings used for nesting and roosting.
Little owl	20 – 40 × 10 – 20	Pale grey, small, loose, often bejewelled by shiny flecks of blue beetle-wing chitin. Sand-coloured when the bird has been feeding on earthworms.
Long-eared owl	20 – 60 × 14 – 27	Pale grey, solid, narrow, with hardish exterior.
Short-eared owl	35 – 70 × 18 – 26	Dark grey, dull (unlike barn owls, with a tendency to fragment).

The Owl

When cats run home and light is come,
And dew is cold upon the ground,
And the far-off stream is dumb,
And the whirring sail goes round,
And the whirring sail goes round;
Alone and warming his five wits,
The white owl in the belfry sits.

When merry milkmaids click the latch,
And rarely smells the new-mown hay,
And the cock hath sung beneath the thatch
Twice or thrice his roundelay,
Twice or thrice his roundelay;
Alone and warming his five wits,
The white owl in the belfry sits.

Alfred, Lord Tennyson (1809–92)

II

The Owls of Britain

THERE HAVE BEEN owls in Britain for a million years. The first fossil record of a native owl comes from the Pastonian Stage, meaning as far back as 1.7 million years ago. As the climate has changed, so has the owl population. The Ice Age and its tundra-like habitat would have favoured birds of the cold treeless plain, such as the snowy owl. From about 10,000 BC the warming of the Holocene period and the emergence of extensive woodland benefited the tawny owl, with as many as 160,000 breeding pairs then in the British Isles (compared to 20,000 pairs now). Barn owls and short-eared owls would have been restricted to open habitats along the coast, with the snowy owl pushed north. With the Anglo-Saxon conquest, and the slow but certain transformation of almost all of Britain into farmland, the barn owl had a heyday. Or hey millennium.

Barn Owl
Tyto alba
Wingspan: 90cm
Weight: 320g (male), 410g (female)
Eggs: white, 4–7, incubation 30–31 days;
occasionally a second clutch is laid

THE BARN OWL is the ghost caught in the car headlights, the sci-fi orb which floats across the field; the Victorian naturalist W. H. Hudson, on noticing 'a vague figure' come out of the evening clouds, considered it looked 'more like a ragged piece of newspaper whirled about the heavens than any living thing'. The front plumage of the barn owl, the male especially, can be almost dazzlingly phosphorescent, like 'burning snow' as J. A. Baker expressed it in *The Hill of Summer* (1969).

Why the brilliant white plumage? White, when seen from below – the prey's-eye view – breaks up the silhouette; it is moonshine, cloud, vagueness.

The gold back of the barn owl is less easy to explain, although it does merge to an extent with dried grass, perhaps providing *Tyto alba* with some degree of deceit when high-flying hawks are about. The seventeenth-century naturalist John Ray postulated that the beauty of butterflies was 'to adorn the world and delight the eyes of man'. It is tempting to conclude that the sun-gold back of the barn owl exists purely for our aesthetic appreciation. Of course, it helps that the barn owl, unlike some other British owls, does not have diverting dayglo yellow or orange eyes, but instead the soft brown eyes of Labrador dogs.

Tyto alba is an owl of open, permanent pasture and the woodland margin. The large wingspan allows the bird to cover immense territory, 250 acres or more a night. Perhaps *the* noiseless flyer, the barn owl's downy edge feathers caress the air into complicit silence. Patrolling is punctuated by rests on posts, fences, trees. When the ear or the eye detects the presence of prey, the owl may hover, kestrel-style.

Barn owls tend to hunt from dusk until about 2am, with a secondary bout of stalking around dawn. The timing of the hunt is far from random; it connects to the activity pattern of the wee timorous beasties on which the owl preys. More than 90 per cent by weight of the barn owl's diet consists of mole, field vole, bank vole, common shrew, pygmy shrew and wood mouse. Birds, frogs, toads and bats comprise the rest.

Like many animals and plants that live in close proximity to man, the barn owl has collected a host of folk names, at least thirty. The bulk of the country names for the barn owl are descriptive of appearance ('silver owl', 'white hoolet', 'white owl', 'yellow owl') or voice ('scritch owl', 'roarer', 'hissing owl', and in Yorkshire it is 'screaming owl'). The familiar 'Billy Wix' and 'Madge Howlet' are clear attempts to make the barn owl less frightening, in the same way that people once called the Devil 'Old Nick'. In the north of Scotland the barn owl was 'Cailleach-oidhche Gheal' ('white old woman of the night').

Breeding barn owls very often choose to nest in farm buildings, hence the name. Other sites include ruined buildings and hollow trees. Their liking for church towers led them to be called 'cherubim' in some parts of the country, 'church owl' in others. They are devoted to tradition, and will use the same locations for years. Nowadays they take readily to nest boxes. As with the other British owls, the breeding season is March–April, but the barn owl (along with the short-eared species) can produce a second clutch.

Eggs are laid on a heap of pellets made up of the indigestible fur, feathers and bones of their prey. The macabre birth-bed is matched by the gruesomeness of the newborn owlets: pink, naked and completely blind. Somehow, the ugly owlets grow up to be beautiful owls with heart-shaped faces and backs of spun gold.

Barn owls have developed a survival system whereby the hungriest chicks eat first, meaning chicks do not waste energy fighting for food. Wise owlets, indeed.

Only when out hunting or asleep are barn owls mute. Nesting barn owls hiss like snakes when disturbed, owlets beg with an asthmatic wheeze, and adults in want of territory or a mate screech. Indisputably, there is something spooky about the barn owl's cry. In Classical myth, Ascalaphus is transformed into a 'screech owl' for tattling about Persephone's eating of pomegranate seeds in the

Underworld; according to Ovid, Ascalaphus became 'the vilest bird; a messenger of grief; the lazy owl; sad omen to mankind'. Shakespeare frequently employed barn owls to dramatic effect, and nowhere better than in *King Henry VI*, Act V, Scene 6, when, at the hour of his murder, King Henry tells Richard of Gloucester, 'The owl shriek'd at thy birth, an evil sign.' Barn owls, frequenters of ruins, were believed to bring ruin by association.

When Shakespeare wrote these words, the national population of barn owls was around its peak. From the mid-nineteenth century the population began to decline. Gamekeepers charged barn owls with the crime of gobbling game chicks, and fashionistas desired *Tyto*'s feathers, head and wings for their toque, a small hat with an upturned brim. One Victorian ornithologist recounted seeing an advertisement in London, 'Wanted at once by a London firm, 1,000 owls.' Later, pesticides took their toll. During the 1960s–80s poisoning from agrichemicals was a major cause of barn owl mortality (as much as 40 per cent in eastern arable areas). The birds would die on their backs, claws grasping at the sky and life, as the chemicals burned their guts. Now, due to its love of farmland and farm buildings, the barn owl is the owl species most at risk from the use of rodenticides. So they still die in slow agony, but breathless from lack of oxygen; most rodenticides thin the blood.

Few farm buildings remain 'unimproved', so there are fewer places for the barn owl to nest. By the same token, rough 'unimproved' grassland, run through with field voles, is also at a premium in the industrialized agriculture that rules Britain's fields. A survey carried out between 1995 and 1997 produced a national estimate of c.4,000 pairs, down from about 12,000 pairs in 1930. Conservation work seems to have stabilized the population. Three-quarters of barn owls now live in man-made nesting boxes.

Tawny Owl
Strix aluco
Wingspan: 100cm
Weight: 400g (male), 430g (female)
Eggs: white, 2–5, incubation 28–30 days

Sweet Suffolk owl, so trimly dight
With feathers, like a lady bright,
Thou sing'st alone, sitting by night,
Te whit, te whoo!
Thy note, that forth so freely rolls,
With shrill command the mouse controls
And sings a song for dying souls.
Te whit, te whoo!

Thomas Vautor (?1580–?1619)

OUR BEST KNOWN, most determinedly nocturnal, most abundant owl, though curiously absent from Ireland and the Isle of Wight. This is the owl after which Brownie troop leaders are named.

The tawny owl is, indeed, tawny – a definite brown, but richly mottled to resemble the trunks and boughs of its arboreal heartland. (The bird's old country names include 'wood owl' and 'beech owl'.)

The tawny is more often heard than seen. The autumnal territorial howling of the male begins in late September once the birds have completed their moult, and the calls increase in frequency until December. The male tawny who has failed to establish a personal fiefdom by late winter, either by superior fighting or calling, is a tawny doomed. The owl will hold his manor until he dies. To maintain territory tawnies will attack trespassing owls – and even foxes and dogs, not to mention humans. Eric Hosking, the famous photographer of birds, lost an eye in a tawny attack. He titled his autobiography *An Eye for a Bird*.

The poet's 'Te whit, te whoo' is actually one owl calling and another (usually a female) chanting the response. It is a duet, not a solo performance.

Also, the contact call is best rendered as *ker-wick*, rather than *te-whit*.

The Reverend C. A. Johns, one of those parson naturalists that England once bred in profusion, instructed readers of *British Birds in Their Haunts*, 1909, that the territorial 'woo' of the owl may 'be imitated so exactly as to deceive even the birds themselves, by forming a hollow with the fingers and the palms of two hands, leaving an opening only between the second joints of the two thumbs, and then by blowing with considerable force down upon the opening thus made, so as to produce the sound *hoo-hoo-hoo-h-o-o-o*'.

William Wordsworth, like many a child, tried his hand at 'talking' to owls, writing in 'There was a Boy', the autobiographical poem about his developing love for nature:

> *There was a Boy; ye knew him well, ye cliffs*
> *And islands of Winander! many a time,*
> *At evening, when the earliest stars began*
> *To move along the edges of the hills,*
> *Rising or setting, would he stand alone,*
> *Beneath the trees, or by the glimmering lake;*
> *And there, with fingers interwoven, both hands*
> *Pressed closely palm to palm and to his mouth*

Uplifted, he, as through an instrument,
Blew mimic hootings to the silent owls
That they might answer him. – And they would shout
Across the watery vale, and shout again,
Responsive to his call, – with quivering peals,
And long halloos, and screams, and echoes loud
Redoubled and redoubled; concourse wild
Of jocund din!

Despite a preference for deciduous wood and thicket, the tawny is adaptable enough to make a home in mature gardens and parkland, meaning that it is the owl most likely to be encountered in the cityscape. The tawny makes its living from small mammals and birds, large insects and frogs.

The tawny is a 'perch and pounce' predator, sitting on a branch to aurally scan the woodland floor for minute scuttling mammals: field voles, bank voles, wood mice, large beetles, birds, and moles, for it is quite the mole-catcher: about 5 per cent of its diet is made up of the little gentlemen in velvet jackets. With a body weight in excess of 430g for an adult female, the tawny is big enough to take young rabbits. At the other end of the menu, the tawny will hop, like an ungainly blackbird, around lawns and fields pulling up earthworms. (In damp weather half the owl's pellets are made up of the fibrous, dirty remains of worms.) Such unfussiness over the menu is another reason for the bird's relative commonness. There are about 20,000 pairs in the United Kingdom.

Like all owls, the tawny is no great home-builder. By choice, the tawny will nest in a cavity in a hollow deciduous tree, preferably wrapped with creeper (which accounts for another country name, 'ivy owl'), with the female scratching a desultory scrape in arboreal debris. Other common accommodation is the abandoned squirrel's drey and corvid's nest. Clutches are usually laid in March. The young are comic balls of grey down, like schoolboys' woolly socks rolled up. On leaving the nest, young tawnies transfer to nearby branches where they loudly demand, with a palpable sense of entitlement, to be fed by their parents.

Most chicks eventually settle to breed within ten or twenty kilometres of the nest site.

Old Brown is an emblem of eternality. Migrant birds bring change; the resident tawny is a reminder of the permanence of the British countryside.

Snowy Owl
Bubo scandiacus
Wingspan: 150cm
Weight: 2kg (male), 2.5kg (female)
Eggs: white, 3–11, incubation 30–33 days

THE SNOWY OWL CAN only be claimed as a British owl because of the birds which bred on Fetlar (Shetland Isles) between 1967 and 1975; in the winter of '76 the male disappeared and breeding stopped. And white beauty was lost from the landscape.

Today, the snowy owl is merely a visitor.

Ice-white, frost-white, the snowy owl appropriately inhabits the Arctic tundra. The near-perfect camouflage means that the snowy owl – also known as the snow owl, or Arctic owl – is often revealed only by a glimpse of its piercing lemon-yellow eyes. The bird's occasional trips south to Britain are caused either by the bitterness of winter in their breeding grounds, or by 'irruptions', crashes in the numbers of the small mammals upon which it feeds. Snowy owls seeking refuge in Britain rarely wander below the Cairngorms. South of the mountains is too warm for snowy owls, even in bleak midwinter.

The adult male is unadulterated white, but youngsters and females are barred and spitted with dark grey or brown (thus camouflaging them in the spartan scrape on rocky ground snowies call a nest). The yellow eyes are ringed with black kohl. Snowy owls rarely perch, but sit to attention on high ground, where they droop their wings, puff out their feathers and lose all bird shape. With a body length in excess of 50cm, the squatting snowy owl resembles a pale, plump cat. On Shetland, the bird is called the 'catyogle'; its felineness is said to frighten cows into producing bloody milk.

Walking, snowies waddle.

From their vantage point, snowy owls swoop, flutter and pounce on prey in a snowstorm of death. But the white terror of the north can also quarter, hover and even glide in, buzzard-fashion. Lemmings, voles, rabbits, and ptarmigan, wader and seagull chicks are staple foods. (The bird has the ability to regulate clutch size according to the preponderance, or not, of prey.) Snowy owls are daytime predators, necessarily so in an environment where it is light for twenty-four hours in summer. The male's calls consist of a grating bark and a booming *hoo*. The female mews, cat-like.

Owls are charismatic, and none more so than the snowy owl. They trail magic in their wake. Small wonder that J. K. Rowling introduced Hedwig the Snowy Owl to the Harry Potter saga in *The Philosopher's Stone*.

Little Owl
Athene noctua
Wingspan: 55cm
Weight: 170g (male), 190g (female)
Eggs: white, 2–5, incubation 27–28 days

LITTLE OWLS WERE FIRST introduced to Britain from Continental Europe by the Yorkshire naturalist

Charles Waterton in 1842. Unfortunately, his habit of giving the birds a warm bath before release led to most dying on the spot. The rest of the freed birds disappeared, never to be seen again.

The first successful introduction was by Mr E. G. B. Meade-Waldo at Stonewell Park, near Edenbridge in Kent, in 1874. The Stonewell Park birds spread throughout the South East, and another enthusiast, Lord Lilford, established the species in the Midlands. The immigrant status of the bird was attested by the foreign place names given it, including 'Dutch owl', 'French owl', 'little Dutch owl'.

By the first decades of the twentieth century, the little owl had conquered almost all of England, together with large slabs of Wales and the Scottish Borders, despite avid persecution by gamekeepers, who accused it of feeding on game chicks. However, one of the earliest investigations by the British Trust for Ornithology proved that the charge was unfounded. About half the bird's diet was – and is – made up of insects, especially cockchafers, beetles, crane flies and earwigs. Game chicks were an insignificant item at mealtime. Our smallest owl is our most catholic in diet, and perhaps our most varied in hunting technique; it will fly up from

the perch, in apparent imitation of the spotted flycatcher, to chase winged things; it will hunt walking on the ground. But prey is generally taken in a pounce off a perch. The little owl is almost completely diurnal.

Flight is undulating, with occasional hovering. When approached at its roadside station of a fence post (for a bird the size of a thrush it sits cockily conspicuous) the little owl will wag its tail and curtsy in a quite manic manner. The commonest call note is a low, pitiful *kiew-kiew*. Other notes in a repertoire more given to volume than tunefulness include *ook*, *ugh* and *eek*.

The bird is, overall, brown in colour with pale and white patches, including frowning eyebrows.

The eyes are clear yellow. This is a bird of copse, hedge and orchard; slow, beefy, contented countryside. The failure of the little owl to colonize Scotland suggests that its breeding range is limited by climatic conditions, and it cannot tolerate the cold, the wet and the snow above Hadrian's Wall. The national population is around 4,000 to 8,500 breeding pairs, according to a study carried out by the British Trust for Ornithology and the Hawk and Owl Trust in the 1990s. Like the tawny, the little owl is ardently territorial on a year-round patch.

A hole in a tree is the little owl's favoured abode, though it has been recorded as using rabbit burrows. Little owls regularly cache food in a larder, the male taking food from the store to the sitting female.

In Greek mythology the little owl was sacred to Pallas Athene (as acknowledged by the bird's scientific name), the goddess of wisdom, and this is one of the prime Western sources for the idea of the 'wise old owl', though nowadays other owls, the tawny in particular, share the reputation for profundity. According to the playwright Aristophanes, Athens, the city devoted to Pallas Athene, was so overflowing with little owls that he wondered, 'And who is it who brings owls to

Athens?' This is the Ancients' version of our saying, 'taking coals to Newcastle'. The little owl became central to Athenian culture. For hundreds of years, from the sixth to the first century BC, Athena and her owl featured on the city state's coins, the goddess on one side, the bird (usually in relief) on the other. Such coins became known colloquially as owls. In *The Birds*, 414 BC, Aristophanes jokes: 'And first of all, what every judge is really keen to have, some owl of Laureium who'll never leave. They'll nest inside your homes, hatch in your purse, and always breed small silver change.' Laureium was the site of the silver mines from whose metal the coins were fashioned.

Little owls are clever in life as well as in Hellenic myth. They are recorded as pouncing on moles working near the surface, but instead of eating the mole's body they leave it and feed on the beetles which throng the corpse.

*Athenian
owl lucky charm*

Short-eared Owl
Asio flammeus
Wingspan: 110cm
Weight: 330g (male), 350g (female)
Eggs: white, 4–14, incubation
24–29 days

FLAMMEUS MEANS 'flame-coloured', and possibly recognizes the reddish hue the bird takes on in the light of the rising or setting sun as it patrols its habitat of mountain, moorland and coastal marsh. This is a bird of open, wet country, as its local names testify: 'moss owl', 'moor owl', 'marsh owl'. The short-eared owl, which flies by day as well as by dusk and by night, is one of our three owls which hunt by quartering (the others being the barn owl and the long-eared owl). Thus it has relatively long, broad wings, which grant it a distinctly assured, cruising flight in which the bird can turn without stalling. When hunting, the short-eared owl fixes its face so as to scan the ground somewhat ahead. I have seen these owls fly at menacingly low height over sedge, a half-metre or less: as soon as prey is spotted, it is seized. Not much escapes the eyes and talons of the short-eared owl. In order to confuse the bird spotter, the short-eared owl will occasionally soar in circles, buzzard-style.

When on the wing, this owl is most easily distinguished from its long-eared near namesake. The short-eared owl has dark wing tips, and a pale trailing edge to the wing. The long-eared version has neither.

The facial disc of the short-eared owl is pale, but ringed by darker feathers. Eyes are yellow. Otherwise, the bird is buff underneath, with a mottled brown back. As with the majority of British owls, the female of the species is heavier than the male.

Disappointingly, the 'ears' which give *Asio flammeus* its common name are no such thing. They are feather tufts, with no function as organs of hearing. They are raised to threaten, otherwise they lie flat to the top of the head.

Voles make up to 83 per cent of the short-eared owl's diet, and it has been calculated that a single bird may eat as many as 6,000 per annum. Where voles do not occur, neither do short-eared owls (thus their absence from Ireland). Periodically, vole plagues break out in hill country, and then the short-eared owl may raise two broods in a season.

Wintering short-eared owls are highly nomadic, and will sometimes congregate on lowland grassland, marsh and fens; a communal roost of 116 birds was found in Norfolk at Christmas in 1972. Such gatherings offer the observer the rare opportunity to use the collective nouns for owls, which are 'parliament' or 'stare'. The numbers of British short-eared owls are boosted by autumn migrants from Scandinavia. On the east coast, the migrations across the North Sea have given rise to the local names 'pilot owl', 'sea owl' and 'woodcock owl' (since the wader arrives simultaneously).

Breeding birds are zealously territorial. The courtship activities of the male short-eared owl are a striking spectacle; there is a hollow *doo doo doo* call, much like the whistle of a far-off steam locomotive, as he flies in a circle before plummeting stone-style while clapping his wings together below his body. Wing-clapping is also used to proclaim territory and warn intruders. A trespassing predator which ignores these warning signs may be encouraged away from the territory by the male feigning injury, thus presenting an easier kill. In extremis short-eared owls will strike at invaders with their talons.

Short-eared owls nest on the ground, usually in tall heather or long grass. Eggs are laid at intervals of one to two days, which results in asynchronous hatching. In periods of dearth, older siblings practise 'Cainism', the eating of younger brothers and sisters. Normal clutch size is around six, but in a good vole year can number fourteen.

Breeding numbers seem to have declined considerably in recent years, more so than other owl species. There are about 2,000 pairs of short-eared owls in the UK, the majority in Scotland. The short-eared owl's predilection for harsh terrain means it was almost certainly one of the first *Strigidae* to colonize Britain following the retreat of the Ice Age glaciers. So, the short-eared owl has been here longer than we have.

Long-eared Owl
Asio otus
Wingspan: 95cm
Weight: 250g (male), 300g (female)
Eggs: white, 3–5, incubation 25–30 days

THE LONG-EARED OWL's heavily prosaic name was invented by Thomas Pennant in 1776, although the first written record of the bird in Britain comes in William Turner's 1544 *Avium praecipuarum, quarum apud Plinium et Aristotelem mentio est, brevis et succincta historia*, where it is called, altogether more charmingly, the 'hornoul'. Country names for the bird are equally evocative: 'horn hoot', 'hornie hoolet', 'tufted owl', 'cat owl'.

But long-eared owl it is to modern ornithology. As with *Asio flammeus* the 'ears' are deterrent devices, or perhaps a means to scare and flush. (When the owl is relaxed, the tufts are flattened backwards.) Certainly, the ears are not aural aids.

The dislike of the Athenians for the long-eared owl – which suffered persecution from devotees of the little owl cult – gave rise to the myth that it is so stupid that, if someone walks around it, the bird,

in turning its head to follow the movement, will wring its own neck. The Athenians used *otus* as a synonym for 'simpleton'.

Plumage is dreary grey, with the typical bars and streaks of a woodland habitué. By day, long-eared owls roost next to a tree trunk with which their cryptic clothing merges. However, on opening their eyes all disguise is lost: the eyes are neon orange.

The long-eared owl is strongly nocturnal, flying low beneath the woodland canopy in a systematic searching of its dominion. Winter feeding ranges approach 100 hectares.

The long-eared owl has a varied repertoire of calls. The male's territorial *hoo-hoo-hoo* is the sound of the party drunk blowing across the top of an empty beer bottle. When alarmed, both sexes utter a barking *kvak, kvak*. As with the short-eared owl, wing-claps are used in courtship.

While widely distributed across Britain, breeding density is concentrated on conifer plantations, though some competition with tawnies over broad-leaved habitat does occur. An advantage the long-eared owl has over Old Brown is its relaxed attitude to accommodation. While the long-eared owl's standard dwelling is a sequestered crow or magpie's nest, the bird will nest on the ground when other sites are in short supply.

Eagle Owl
Bubo bubo
Wingspan: 180cm
Weight: 4kg (female)
Eggs: white, 2–4, incubation 34–36 days.

WHETHER THE EAGLE OWL is a truly British bird is a matter of debate. Although the bird has bred in northern England since the 1990s, these eagle owls have been aviary escapees (the bird has been popular with falconers since the 1600s) or immigrants from across the North Sea. That said, fragments of leg bone found at Meare Lake in Somerset indicate the bird was certainly present here around 2000 BC. So, the eagle owl has a claim to be part of the native fauna. In a word, it has been unintentionally 're-wilded' into Britain.

Bubo bubo is unmistakable, a barrel-shaped giant of an owl with prominent ear tufts and tangerine eyes. A heavy female can weigh as much as 4kg. They are as loud as they are big. The advertising call of the male eagle owl is a reverberating *ooo*. On a quiet night in winter, when the ground is hard with frost, the call can be heard rolling over the earth for two miles or so. The female screams, in a manner reminiscent of a vixen, to make contact, or to demand food from her mate. During courtship, the male and female may duet; the male signals potential breeding sites by emitting staccato clicks as he scratches at a shallow depression. Favoured nest sites are ledges and cave entrances on cliffs. No nesting material is added. Eagle owls often pair for life.

Laying generally begins in late winter, early spring. One clutch per year is laid. After the young become independent in early autumn, and have departed the homeland (or been driven off), the male begins to sing and inspect potential nesting sites. And so the reproductive cycle starts anew.

Eagle owls are adaptable birds. They will take prey on the ground or in flight, and will eat anything made of flesh, from beetles to roe deer fawns, that they can kill. Analysis of the pellets from eagle owls in the Peak District and the Forest of Bowland indicates a diet dominated by rabbit, mountain hare, pheasant, red grouse, stoat, grey squirrel and, the spines notwithstanding, hedgehog. Also on the diet record are cat, lamb, calf, other owls and raptors. The eagle owls in the Forest of Bowland killed and ate three hen harriers, one of the country's rarest and most heavily protected species.

The eagle owl is an apex predator. The bird has no natural enemies, and can live for up to twenty years in the wild. In captivity, the bird will reach sixty years of age.

Owl Visitors

Just three other owls occur in Britain, all three vagrants of varying frequency.

Common Scops Owl *Otus scops*

IN APRIL–JUNE the scops sometimes overshoots its southern European breeding grounds on its migration back from its winter quarters in sub-Saharan Africa. When it does arrive here it is often exhausted. This is a small owl, the size of a song thrush. The plumage is the usual owly faux bark. The ear tufts, when raised, make it look like a mini long-eared owl. Eyes are a staring yellow. When afraid, the scops 'thins' by compressing its feathers, in an attempt to be overlooked.

A nocturnal insect-eater, the scops is often attracted to house lights to capture the moths fluttering there.

Northern Hawk Owl *Surnia ulula*

A VERY SCARCE vagrant, with just nine reputable records. The species is distributed around the North Pole and is highly nomadic, only making 'irruptive' excursions into central Europe, and occasionally into Britain, when rodent populations crash. As the bird's name suggests, it resembles a hawk, having a long tapered tail. It flies like a hawk too, with a mix of slow wingbeats and long glides. The eyes are brilliant yellow, and the facial disc is heavily outlined with a sooty black ring.

Tengmalm's Owl *Aegolius funereus*

SIMILAR IN SIZE to a little owl, Tengmalm's come across in small numbers in autumns when Scandinavian owls are forced to relocate because of bad weather or bad prey numbers. Since 1950 there have been only a handful of certified sightings. The species was added to the British list in 1812, at Morpeth, Northumberland. A shy, nocturnal owl, it is one of the *Strigidae* that possess an asymmetric skull to amplify hearing.

Tengmalm was a Swedish naturalist. The bird is also known as the boreal owl, and Richardson's owl, after Scottish ornithologist Sir John Richardson. *Funereus*, of course, is Latin for funeral. A bird, then, of ill omen. The Cree of North America believed that the boreal owl's whistles were summons from the spirits. If a person answered with a similar whistle and did not hear a response, then he would soon die.

The Owl

In the hollow tree, in the old grey tower,
The spectral Owl doth dwell;
Dull, hated, despised, in the sunshine hour,
But at dusk, – he's abroad and well!
Not a bird of the forest e'er mates with him;
All mock him outright, by day;
But at night, when the woods grow still and dim,
The boldest will shrink away!
  O, when the night falls, and roosts the fowl,
  Then, then, is the reign of the Horned Owl!

And the Owl hath a bride, who is fond and bold,
And loveth the wood's deep gloom;
And, with eyes like the shine of the moonstone cold,
She awaiteth her ghastly groom!
Not a feather she moves, not a carol she sings,
As she waits in her tree, so still;
But when her heart heareth his flapping wings,
She hoots out her welcome shrill!
  O – when the moon shines, and dogs do howl,
  Then, then is the joy of the Horned Owl!

Mourn not for the Owl, nor his gloomy plight!
The Owl hath his share of good:
If a prisoner he be in the broad day-light,
He is Lord in the dark green-wood!
Nor lonely the bird, nor his ghastly mate.
They are each unto each a pride;
Thrice fonder perhaps, since a strange dark fate
Hath rent them from all beside!
  So, when the night falls, and dogs do howl,
  Sing, Ho! for the reign of the Horned Owl!
    We know not alway
    Who are kings by day,
  But the King of the night is the bold brown Owl!

Barry Cornwall (Bryan Waller Procter), 1787–1874

III

Humans and Owls

A wise old owl sat in an oak,
The more he saw the less he spoke,
The less he spoke the more he heard,
Why can't we all be like that wise old bird?

English nursery rhyme

THERE IS A CAVE in the Ardèche in France called the Grotte Chauvet. Early man was early there. It is a 'Paleolithic site of habitation'. The walls of the cave are decorated with prehistoric art, including an incised image of an owl. This 30,000-year-old, 33cm-high carving on the ochre of the Chauvet wall is the oldest known depiction of an owl. At another prehistoric site, the Grotta Romanelli on Italy's Salento peninsula, archaeologists have found butchering marks on the bones of an owl. Given the pathetically small amount of meat on an owl, it is a fair conjecture that the bird was killed in some sacrificial rite rather than a fit of hunger. Back in France, at the Grotte de Bourrouilla, near Arancou, occupied c.1100–9000 BC, the remains of at least fifty-three snowy owls have been found. Here there is no doubt. The butchering shows the considered removal of feathers.

Feather decorations are rife in hunter-gatherer societies, as we know from the North American Indians, and the tribes of the Amazon and Papua New Guinea.

Once more, for emphasis. At the famous Lascaux caves in the Dordogne there is a picture of an owl atop a pole.

Owls feature in every major culture from the Stone Age onwards. Invariably, the owl's cry and nocturnal habits connect it with death, or ill-fortune, and quite possibly both. Mesopotamian tablets from 2300 BC depict the goddess Lilith as 'winged, bird-footed, and typically accompanied by owls', a significant association because Lilith was Sumeria's goddess of the end of things. In China the belief that the owl is the harbinger of death gripped the mind for millennia; on the other side of the world, the Apache feared owls and said if you dreamed about an owl it was a sign of death approaching. According to the Roman writer

Virgil, the long keening of an owl foretold Dido's suicide. In his *Natural History* (AD 77) Pliny the Elder noted a superstition whereby an owl flying in a city 'prognosticates some fearful misfortune'. When an owl was observed in Rome's Capitol building the citizens 'made general processions to appease the wrath of the Gods'. Credulous Romans, if they heard an owl, would, in an attempt to negate the coming misfortune, kill the bird and cremate it. A millennium and a half on and Edmund Spenser in *The Faerie Queen* declared owls the 'hateful messengers of heavy . . . tidings'. Always one for utilizing the dramatic possibilities of the owl, Shakespeare has Puck say of the barn owl in *A Midsummer Night's Dream* that the bird's screeching 'Puts the wretch that lies in woe, in remembrance of a shroud'.

Not to be outdone by the Bard, Sir Walter Scott wrote:

Birds of omen dark and foul,
Night-crow, raven, bat, and owl,
Leave the sick man to his dream –
All night long he heard your scream.

A Suffolk superstition which lingered into the Victorian age held that an owl flying past the window of a room in which a sick person lay meant that death was near. One name for the owl in Welsh is *aderyn corff*. Corpse bird.

For all of the artistic fantasizing of Scott, shamans, poets and playwrights, the owl's link with death has a glaringly simple explanation. Most people die at night, when the biorhythms are ebbing. Also, those staying awake on the death-bed vigil, super-sensitized by emotion, are particularly conscious of the owl hooting in the night.

The owl is the messenger of death, but it is also the guide to the other side. The Lascaux pole owl may well have indicated a superstition that the owl flew the spirit to the other world. During the Shang dynasty (c.1500–1045 BC) in China, owl figures were placed in graves, most plausibly to escort the dead to the afterlife. Numerous Native American tribes viewed the owl as a spiritual ferryman: an owl feather placed in the hand of a dying person in the Pima tribe allows the bird to lead the deceased on the long journey to the other side. If the owl can see at night, it can, 'primitive' people deduced, see through the vapours, darkness and mysteries of the journey to the land of the dead souls.

With its nocturnality and its association with death, the owl slipped easily into becoming a thing of outright evil. Chinese children born on the day of the owl, the summer solstice, were considered to have a matricidal personality (something which stems from the Taoist belief that young owls would pluck out their mother's eyes or even devour her). In Malaya, where owls are known as *burung hantu* or 'ghost birds', they were believed to eat babies. Likewise, in Ancient Rome there was a popular superstition that witches could turn themselves into owls and suck the blood of sleeping babies.

The Bible is full of laments about owls, with the tone set by Deuteronomy 14 and the injunction 'Thou shalt not eat any abominable thing'; the owl is high on the list of the horrible. The Old Testament's loathing of owls impacted on Christian conceptions concerning the bird. In thirteenth-century Europe, the owl was a member of a demonic trio, alongside the monkey and the goat. Some medieval Christian theologians contended that the owl, as a being of the night, was an emblem of the Jews, because they preferred the blackness of their belief to the light of Christianity. In the myths of North America, the owl is frequently employed as a bogeyman to scare children into good behaviour, as in the Chippewa tale about a boy called Redfeather, a little vandal, who shot at all the animals with a bow and arrow, until an owl kidnapped him:

> The owl flew across the lake to his island, and up into an old oak tree where the nest of baby owls were.
>
> He put Redfeather down there, and told his babies, 'When you get big enough to eat meat, you shall eat Redfeather.' The little owls were quite excited at this. Then the owl flew away. The next day, the owl called to the crane and the other birds and said, 'When your babies are old enough we'll have a feast of Redfeather. I have him imprisoned in my oak tree.' So Redfeather was kept a prisoner, and he cried, but he couldn't get down.

Eventually, a feast organized by the boy's grandfather in the owl's honour secured Redfeather's release.

The most famous British myth about owls is contained in the collection of Welsh, pre-Christian Celtic stories known as the *Mabinogion*. In the book of 'Math fab Mathonwy' ('Math, son of Mathonwy') the heroic tribal chief Lleu Llaw Gyffes has a taboo placed on him by his mother Arianrhod by which he may never have a human wife. To counter the curse, the magicians Math and Gwydion take 'the flowers of the oak, and the flowers of the broom, and the flowers of the meadowsweet, and from those they conjured up the fairest and most beautiful maiden anyone had ever seen. And they baptized her in the way that they did at that time, and named her Blodeuwedd.' Or 'Flowerface'.

Of course, it all goes tragically wrong. When Lleu is away on business, Blodeuwedd has an affair with Gronw Pebr, lord of Penllyn. The two lovers conspire to murder Lleu, but he escapes by assuming the form of an eagle. He then takes his revenge on the conspirators. Blodeuwedd flees with her entourage, but they fall into a lake:

> And they were all drowned except Blodeuwedd herself, and her Gwydion overtook. And he said unto her, 'I will not slay thee, but I will do unto thee worse than that. For I will turn thee into a bird; and because of the shame thou hast done unto Lleu Llaw Gyffes, thou shalt never show thy face in the light of day henceforth; and that through fear of all the other birds. For it shall be their nature to attack thee, and to chase thee from wheresoever they may find thee. And thou shalt not lose thy name, but shalt be always called Blodeuwedd.' Now Blodeuwedd is an owl in the language of this present time, and for this reason

is the owl hateful unto all birds. And even now the owl is called Blodeuwedd.

Blodeuwedd, then, is the original femme fatale.

There is no certainty over the source for the belief in the wisdom of the owl, but it is probably prehistoric. We are wise, we are *Homo sapiens*. The owl has a human face. Ergo, the owl must be wise. Additionally, the owl is conspicuously solitary, like the hermit seeking truth.

Biology is a disappointment here, because the crow family are indisputably cleverer than owls.

Nonetheless, it is the owl that has captured the imagination as the sage in feathers. The Ancient Greeks gave the notion a rocket-boost with the cult of Athena (see p. 45), which maintained that both the goddess and the little owl were *glaukopis* (bright-eyed); it was their superior eyesight that allowed them to penetrate the real dark and the metaphorical dark of ignorance. From Ancient Greece, a distinct thread hailing the wisdom of owls spools into Western culture. In the fable 'The Mice and the Owl' by Jean de La Fontaine (1621–95), the owl has even achieved the ability to think logically:

A thing which with the air of fable,
Is true as is the interest-table.
A pine was by a woodman fell'd,
Which ancient, huge, and hollow tree
An owl had for his palace held –
A bird the Fates had kept in fee,
Interpreter to such as we.
Within the caverns of the pine,
With other tenants of that mine,
Were found full many footless mice,
But well provision'd, fat, and nice.
The bird had bit off all their feet,
And fed them there with heaps of wheat.
That this owl reason'd, who can doubt?

Wol in A. A. Milne's much-loved *Winnie-the-Pooh*, published in 1926, is clearly of Athenian descent.

Ancient Greece was also the wellspring for other Western notions about owls. The owl for Athenians was a totem of good fortune. Their proverb 'there goes an owl' indicated belief in victory. One Athenian general in 310 BC, in order to raise the morale of the troops, kept an owl hidden in the baggage train; when released on to the battlefield it emboldened the troops, who duly routed the

Carthaginians. The 'luckiness' of the Athenian owl spread far and wide; the American president Theodore Roosevelt carried an Athenian owl lucky charm. Even today the owl is the main lucky charm for the inhabitants of the Mediterranean island of Menorca, while weddings in Scotland sometimes have a live owl delivering the rings to the best man.

In Ancient Greece the protean Athene also symbolized moderation; she was the counterbalance to Dionysian excess. Consequently, owls were believed, if touched or consumed, to be able to cure drunkenness. This is an obvious instance of sympathetic magic, by which an animal or plant possessing certain features is utilized in the expectation the power will be transferred to the human patient. The owl looks sober; consequently its temperance can be passed on.

If it was good enough for the Ancient Greeks, it was good enough for the civilizations of Western Europe for millennia. The belief that eating owls' eggs would prevent drunkenness lasted until the nineteenth century, at least. Indeed, ancient belief in the curative properties of the owl for all manner of human ailments cascaded down the centuries. Pliny the Elder listed boiled owl fat as a means to rid the body of sores. Salted owl flesh was a remedy for gout (believed to be brought on by over-indulgence in alcohol). The fifteenth-century medical compendium *Hortus Sanitatis* records that a treatment for madness included the placing of an owl's ashes on the lunatic's eyes. Owl's blood was said to eradicate headlice. Dried and pounded owl's crop would cure colic. Powdered burnt feet of an owl, taken internally, was a specific against snake bite. In Yorkshire, broth made from the hooting bird was used as a cure for whooping cough. Elsewhere, owl soup was a remedy for epilepsy. (As owls are so calm and composed, it was believed that the frenzied movements of the epileptic fit would be stilled by imbibing owl essence.) Perhaps the weirdest 'medicine of owl' comes from Germany, where it was supposed that the transmission of rabies via the bite of an infected dog could be prevented by placing the heart and right foot of an owl under your left armpit.

Superstitious uses of owl did not end with medicine. The heart of an owl, placed on the left breast of a sleeping woman, would make her disclose her secrets – an early truth drug. The barn owl was a weather diviner; a screeching barn owl indicated cold weather or a storm. If heard during foul weather, a change in the weather was at hand.

In Glamorgan hooting owls foretold snow. Or a maiden losing her virginity. Until the nineteenth century in Britain owls were nailed over the barn and house portal to ward off lightning and the 'evil eye', meaning misfortune.

A more enlightened use of the owl in Britain was rodent-catching. Medieval barns were always made with an ingress for owls, often with a stone perch, to enable them to enter and pick off the vermin. The manufacturers of modern agricultural buildings tend to be less wise.

The Owl and the Nightingale c. 1200–15

The Owl and the Nightingale is a Middle English poem detailing an altercation between the eponymous birds, as overheard by the poem's narrator. When he first happens upon them, the Nightingale is perched on a blossom-covered branch, and the Owl is sitting on a bough overgrown with ivy. The Nightingale begins the argument by insulting the Owl's physique, 'song' and habits:

> Then thou art loathsome to behold: and loathsome art thou in many ways. Thy body is short: thy neck is thin: thy head is bigger than all thy body. Thine eyes

also are coal-black and broad, just as if they were painted with woad: and with them thou glarest, as if thou wouldst devour all that thou mayst clutch by means of thy claws. Thy bill is strong and sharp and hooked, like to an awl crooked in shape: and with this bill thou clackest continually – which, indeed, is one of thy songs … Thou lurkest by day and fliest at night, showing by this thou art unnatural. And thou art horrible and dirty as well – I refer to thy nest and to thy foul brood, in which thou dost rear a most filthy family. Well knowest thou what they do therein: they defile their nest up to their chins, sitting meanwhile as if they were blind. And of this matter men make a proverb: 'Cursed be the creature that defiles its own nest.'

The Owl suggests to the Nightingale that it fly out into the open to continue the argument, but the Nightingale, sensing a trick ('Thou hast talons mighty and strong, with which thou dost squeeze like a pair of tongs'), refuses. Instead, the Nightingale proposes 'a proper trial, using fair and friendly words', and recommends Master Nicholas de Guildford (in all probability the author of the poem) as the judge. Although a playboy in his youth, Nicholas is now a serious man, and can adjudicate on the birds' claims as in a court of law. However, the Nightingale immediately goes on to shame the Owl for the gloomy screeches she produces, and stresses that she is 'unnatural' because she prefers night over day:

> The Nightingale, meanwhile, was ready for action: her wit was drawn from many sources. 'Owl!' she said, 'tell me truly: why behavest thou in unnatural fashion? Thou singest at night and not by day: and thy whole song is a lament, with which thou dost terrify all who hear thy noise. Thou shriekest and hootest to thy mate in a way that is awful to hear: so that to men, both wise and foolish, it seems not that thou singest but that thou dost weep. Then, too, thou fliest at night and not by day: at this I wonder, and well I may. For everything that shuns what is right loves the darkness and hates the light. And everything that inclines to evil likes the darkness for its deed. A wise saying there is, which, though unpolished, is often heard on the lips of men, for King Alfred said and wrote it: "A man shuns that which knows him to be foul." And so it is, I suppose, with thee: for ever dost thou fly at night. And another thing I have in mind: thou hast at night the clearest vision, whereas by day thou art stone-blind, seeing neither tree nor stream. In the day-time thou art blind and sightless: and of this, men make a parable. "So it is with the

wicked man who sees naught to any good purpose, and is so full of evil tricks that no man is able to deceive him. He knows well the way of darkness and avoids the way of light." Thus do all of thy kindred: of the light they have no care.'

The Owl's retort is a defence of owl kind:

'Keep quiet and let me speak: and I shall be revenged on thee. And listen how I can clear myself with truthful words without ado. Thou sayest that I hide by day: and this I in no way deny. But listen and I'll tell thee why – the whole reason for the same. I have a strong and sturdy beak, good claws as well both sharp and long, as befits one of the hawk-tribe. It is my joy, my delight as well, that I live in accord with Nature: and for this no man can blame me. In me it is plainly seen that by Nature's laws I am so fierce: and that is why I am hated by the little birds, that fly near the ground and in the thickets, as they twitter around me, uttering their cries and bringing their flocks in force against me. But I prefer to take a rest, sitting quietly in my nest: for I should be no better off if I put them to rout with scolding or with chattering, or by using bad language as the shepherds do. Nor do I care to bandy words with such spit-fires: and therefore I keep them at a distance.

'But thou dost bring forward another shameful charge – that I am defective in my eyes. Thou sayest that because I fly at night, I am unable to see by day. But there thou liest! for it is clear that I have good eyesight, since no darkness is so dim as to prevent my seeing.'

The Owl also declares her attributes, which are helpful to mankind: 'But I can render services of a useful kind: for I can protect the dwellings of men. And my services are very valuable, for I help with the food of men. I can catch mice in the barns: and also in church during the hours of darkness. For the house of God is dear to me: I love to cleanse it of loathsome mice.'

The Nightingale claims she too is helpful to the Church, since her songs invoke the glories of Heaven, and encourage churchgoers to be more devout. The Owl counters that before people can reach Heaven, they must repent their sins. Her mournful, haunting song makes them reconsider their decisions:

'My advice is therefore that those who yearn for the king of heaven should get ready to weep rather than sing, since there is no man who is free from sin. Therefore, a man, before he goes hence, must make due atonement with tears and with weeping, so that what before was sweet may henceforth be bitter. And, God knows, I help mankind in this matter. I sing to men no foolishness. My song is of yearning and partly of lament, so that man in consequence may take heed to himself and bewail his transgressions: with my singing I urge him to groan for his misdeeds.'

The Nightingale, not to be outdone, claims that the Owl is of no real use except when dead, since farmers use her corpse as a scarecrow. The Owl gives a positive twist to the charge by inferring that she helps men even after death:

'Thou sayest that I am hateful to men, that every man is angry with me, and, attacking me with stones and sticks, they beat me and break me all to pieces: and, moreover, when they have me slain, that they hang me high upon their hedges to scare away magpies and also crows, from the seeds that are sown near by. Though this be true, it is also true that I render them service; for them indeed did I shed my blood. I do them good by my death – which for thee is very difficult. For although thou liest dead and shrivelling up, thy death nevertheless serves no purpose! I know not in the least what use thou art: for thou art only a miserable thing. But if the life is shot out of me, yet even so may I do some good. I can be fastened to a small stick in the thick-set of a wood, so that man can attract and capture little birds, and thus obtain through my help roast meat for his food.'

This is not refutation as far as the Nightingale is concerned, and she calls other birds to jeer at the Owl. The Owl, in turn, threatens to assemble her predatory friends, but before the tension can escalate further, the Wren descends to quiet the quarrel.

The poem is an allegory in which the penitential Owl represents the Church, while the Nightingale is an advocate for secular pleasure and the court. What makes the poem fascinating for ornithologists is the degree of original observation. The plumage of the owl is described accurately, as is the 'mobbing' of owls. Their usefulness in taking mice from within farm buildings is recognized. The myth of the blindness of the owl is refuted. Equally, the poem is evidence of just how deep-seated are other myths about owls, particularly their inclination to evil because of their liking of the night.

The Owl

Downhill I came, hungry, and yet not starved;
Cold, yet had heat within me that was proof
Against the north wind; tired, yet so that rest
Had seemed the sweetest thing under a roof.

Then at the inn I had food, fire, and rest,
Knowing how hungry, cold, and tired was I.
All of the night was quite barred out except
An owl's cry, a most melancholy cry.

Shaken out long and clear upon the hill,
No merry note, nor cause of merriment,
But one telling me plain what I escaped
And others could not, that night, as in I went.

And salted was my food, and my repose,
Salted and sobered, too, by the bird's voice
Speaking for all who lay under the stars,
Soldiers and poor, unable to rejoice.

Edward Thomas (1878–1917)

Thomas wrote 'The Owl' in February 1915 while he havered over whether to fight in the Great War. It is the owl, the messenger bird, that tells him to enlist. He died in the Battle of Arras, on 9 April 1917.

The Lord of the Night

DUSK FLOODS between the trees, drowning the wood in darkness. Some jackdaws tumble overhead, 'jack-jacking' in the last of the light.

No other birds sing. It is too late in the day.

From somewhere ahead Old Brown the tawny owl calls *ker-wick*. He has clocked the coming of night. The countryside has no need of watches. The robin signals dawn, the tawny owl calls dusk.

Faster. Deeper into the wood, the trees stepping aside for me.

Ker-wick. Close by.

Above my head, a slight waft of air, such as you would get from a coy Georgian lady's fan at a ball. Old Brown is aloft.

I see him. Just: a leaf blown through the pillars of the autumn oaks.

Far ahead, I can hear the cattle moving; the crackle of branches under hooves, the slow drumbeat of massive beasts moving. It is some sound, I tell you; it is the sound of aurochs in wildwood.

Onwards, following the faint ink line of the clay path as it squiggles between the dulled obstacles of beech, sweet chestnut, oak.

Something fluttering in the air to my right. Old Brown again? A bat? But the more the blindness, the greater the sense of smell. The days of frost have locked down the usual odours of woodland, so I detect the evidential dab of tobacco scent in the air easily enough.

Old Brown has a definite odour; his favoured roost is in a rotten ash, and something of the crumbling, musty timber clings to his plumage.

On, now past the larch where Old Brown coughs up his grey, felty pellets. Gingerly, with sticks, I sometimes prise apart these little cabinets of macabre curiosities with their gut-bleached bones. They pack surprises. In one pellet I found the skull of a newt. How Macbeth's witches would have loved that.

Dark now: the quarter moon failing to break through the cloud that came on the western sky.

From the far side of the wood: *Hoo-hoo-hoo-h-o-o-o. Hoo-hoo-hoo-h-o-o-o.*

Night musick: the hoot of a tawny.

Is there an index of owl happiness? A gauge for measuring owly content? I think so. For the four years we have been managing Three Acre Wood, Old Brown's wives have produced steadily bigger clutches. Two eggs. Three eggs. Four eggs. And this year, five eggs.

The reason for the increasing size of the clutches is that we have improved the tawnies' food supply by reducing the invasive bramble, nature's barbed wire, which covered the woodland floor. Old Brown was simply unable to penetrate the bramble when out hunting.

I say 'we' have reduced the bramble, but the work has been done by the beasts, by the hooves and the teeth of the cows, pigs and sheep. More than half the wood now is picture-book, textbook woodland floor of leaf litter, fallen boughs, and glades. No longer does Old Brown live on the margins, or need to fly from this wood to another wood and another. His meals of shrew and mice scurry in their hundreds around his home.

On, on, to the top of the wood, and there are the cattle, out in the towers of oak, four red poll cows, black prehistoric shapes lying in a ragged circle watching for the sabre-toothed tigers of bovine nightmares.

The cattle are checked, and all present and correct. My job as the good cattle-herder is done for the night.

But I have lost my sense of where Old Brown is.

The wood (to my ears) has slept into silence. Old Brown, however, can hear the turn of a leaf . . . and the scamper of rabbit on grass.

The scream comes from only yards away; it is a scream that terrifies the night. I and the little animals in the wood stop and hold our breath.

The distinctive, high-pitched wail is well known to us wood folk. If I was cold before, I am colder now.

The Lord of the Night has killed a rabbit, and its death is musick to his ears.

BRITISH AND INTERNATIONAL OWL SOCIETIES

BOCN – THE BARN OWL CONSERVATION NETWORK
www.bocn.org
*A network of specialist voluntary advisers working to
promote a barn owl-friendly national habitat along with
the installation of nest boxes.*
c/o Wildlife Conservation Partnership,
2 Mill Walk, Wheathampstead, Herts AL4 8DT
Tel: 0845 051 0344
Email: bocnenquiries@aol.com

THE BARN OWL TRUST
www.barnowltrust.org.uk
*'Founded in 1988, the Barn Owl Trust is a small
national charity working very hard to conserve one of
the most beautiful birds on Earth.'*
Waterleat, Ashburton, Devon TQ13 7HU
Tel/Fax: 01364 653026
Email: info@barnowltrust.org.uk

THE BARN OWL CENTRE OF GLOUCESTERSHIRE
www.barnowl.co.uk
Netheridge Farm, Netheridge Close, Hempsted,
Gloucester GL2 5LE
Tel: 01452 383999

HAWK AND OWL TRUST
hawkandowl.org
Founded in 1969, the Hawk and Owl Trust is dedicated to 'conserving owls and other birds of prey in the wild; increasing knowledge and appreciation of them through: creation and management of nesting, roosting and feeding habitats; practical research; wildlife reserves; education centres and outreach projects'.
Turf Moor Road, Sculthorpe, Fakenham, Norfolk NR21 9GN
Tel: 01328 850590
Email: *enquiries@hawkandowl.org*

HEREFORD OWL RESCUE
herefordowlrescue.co.uk
'Our aim is to rescue owls, which were being neglected in favour of other birds of prey by existing rescue centres.'
Tel: 01544 318974
or in an 'Owl Emergency' **07977 948102**
Email: *herefordowl@herefordowlrescue.co.uk*

INTERNATIONAL CENTRE FOR BIRDS OF PREY
www.icbp.org
Aims and objectives: 'The conservation of all birds of prey and their habitats through public education and captive breeding. Treatment and rehabilitation of wild injured birds of prey. Research for understanding the health and conservation of all birds of prey. To preserve the longstanding heritage and history of British and

Worldwide falconry.' The centre is open to the general public for 10 months of the year, plus parts of December for Owl Evenings.
Boulsdon House, Newent, Gloucestershire GL18 1JJ
Tel: 01531 820286
Email: info@icbp.org

INTERNATIONAL OWL SOCIETY
international-owl-society.com
UK-based society formed in 1996 'intended as a worldwide forum for anyone with an interest in owls'.
5 Sorrel Close, Braiswick, Colchester C04 5UL
Email: john.a.gray@btinternet.com

THE SUFFOLK OWL SANCTUARY
www.owl-help.org.uk
Established as a registered charity in 2001, the Sanctuary 'operates a comprehensive facility for the care and rehabilitation of owls from the region, and the promotion of owl conservation throughout the UK and beyond'.
Stonham Barns, Pettaugh Road,
Stonham Aspal IP14 6AT
Tel: 03456 807897
Email: info@owl-help.org.uk

UK LITTLE OWL PROJECT
www.littleowlproject.uk
Dedicated to UK little owl research and conservation.

WORLD OF OWLS
www.worldofowls.com
'Northern Ireland's Premier Owl, Bird of Pre
Animal Conservation Centre'.
Randalstown Forest, 32 Mt Shalgus Lane,
County Antrim BT41 3LE
Tel: 028 9447 2307
Email: admin@worldofowls.com

WORLD OWL TRUST
www.owls.org
'The World Owl Trust works on owl conservat
National and International scale, and we hav
in many countries around the world.'
Millstones, Bootle, Cumbria LA19 5TJ
Tel: 01229 718080
Email: jen@owls.org

Worldwide falconry.' The centre is open to the general public for 10 months of the year, plus parts of December for Owl Evenings.
Boulsdon House, Newent, Gloucestershire GL18 1JJ
Tel: 01531 820286
Email: info@icbp.org

INTERNATIONAL OWL SOCIETY
international-owl-society.com
UK-based society formed in 1996 'intended as a worldwide forum for anyone with an interest in owls'.
5 Sorrel Close, Braiswick, Colchester CO4 5UL
Email: john.a.gray@btinternet.com

THE SUFFOLK OWL SANCTUARY
www.owl-help.org.uk
Established as a registered charity in 2001, the Sanctuary 'operates a comprehensive facility for the care and rehabilitation of owls from the region, and the promotion of owl conservation throughout the UK and beyond'.
Stonham Barns, Pettaugh Road,
Stonham Aspal IP14 6AT
Tel: 03456 807897
Email: info@owl-help.org.uk

UK LITTLE OWL PROJECT
www.littleowlproject.uk
Dedicated to UK little owl research and conservation.

WORLD OF OWLS
www.worldofowls.com
'Northern Ireland's Premier Owl, Bird of Prey and Exotic Animal Conservation Centre'.
Randalstown Forest, 32 Mt Shalgus Lane, Randalstown, County Antrim BT41 3LE
Tel: 028 9447 2307
Email: admin@worldofowls.com

WORLD OWL TRUST
www.owls.org
'The World Owl Trust works on owl conservation on a National and International scale, and we have members in many countries around the world.'
Millstones, Bootle, Cumbria LA19 5TJ
Tel: 01229 718080
Email: jen@owls.org